T5-AFM-812

Doris' Red
Spaces

9
SIGNED
3

For my CECIA,

my poetic Sister.

♡

Doris' Red Spaces

Gretchen Primack

4/14

Mayapple Press 2014

© Copyright 2014 by Gretchen Primack

Published by   **MAYAPPLE PRESS**
362 Chestnut Hill Rd.
Woodstock, NY 12498
www.mayapplepress.com

ISBN 978-1-936419-33-3
Library of Congress Control Number: 2014932135

ACKNOWLEDGMENTS

Some of these poems have appeared in (occasionally in an earlier form):

Antioch Review: Matter; *Best New Poets 2006* (Meridian Press): Colors; *Big City Lit:* Parting; *Bloom :* Space Exploration; *Borderlands: Texas Poetry Review:* Space; *Brooklyn Review:* 16mm; *Cimarron Review:* Space Exploration; *Columbia Poetry Review:* 1988 and June; *The Cortland Review:* August and Somewhere Along the Way; *Crab Creek Review:* Great Blasket Island; *Entelechy:* Patient S. to Doris; *FIELD:* Doris (Cardiology 14 E), Colors, Red Pail Market, March, and Doris Out of Love; *5 AM:* Seventh Grade; *Global City Review:* Spring Night; *Hanging Loose:* Doris in Love; *Hungry as We Are: An Anthology of Washington Area Poets*: Space Exploration; *Jewish Currents:* October; *Lumina:* Of the Girl; *Mad Hatter Review:* Doris Can Juggle, Forest Floor, July, and The Crush; *The Massachusetts Review:* Bird; *Measure:* The Housewife; *Open City:* It Is Green; *The Paris Review:* The Real World, Child, and September; *Ploughshares:* You Are a Prince; *Poet Lore:* Over and Michael Kleiman; *Prairie Schooner:* Midnight and Smoushound; *Re:Union:* Bride; *Rhino:* Avenue; *Sulphur River Literary Review:* Tony's Goodbye and The Drawbridge; *Tampa Review:* The Albert Einstein Memorial

Some of these poems are included in the chapbook *The Slow Creaking of Planets* (Finishing Line Press, 2007).

Cover art by Gus Mueller. Cover designed by Judith Kerman. Book designed and typeset by Amee Schmidt with cover titles in Optima and poem titles and text in Adobe Caslon Pro. Author photo courtesy of Deborah DeGraffenreid.

Contents

Hollows

I like the one where a crib's
supposed to be, the pastels

that become primaries. That
space is swept space: I burst

a bright red filling every
month and leave it at that.

Other spaces need filling
in around it, though, the

stomach, the cozy napped
fabric of the lungs, the heart,

all the unnamed brittle
gourds rattling their cavities,

thimbles and duffels to fill,
such a tall and tiring order,

hat and shoe boxes to fill
or else feel alone, every

hollow mysterious, this one
about sex and that one about

god and those others trying
to fill with fancy birds,

downright silly
ones, downright painted.

August

All right, Doris, it's a perfect dusk
for a walk. I've never seen
such a fuzzed mushroom. A few
yards ahead, I've never known one
to show so much gill.

Doris, your profile is dreadful
in the violet light. Leave beauty
to the newts, and these dozen
water bugs, wrestling
with their own bridges
and dams.

The clouds look
like shovelfuls of dirt.
I'm so exhausted, it's as if
I did that landscaping.

No, Doris, not from anything
in particular: just
being here,
and I know you know
what I mean.

Avenue

I'm tired. Men can *hey baby*
all they want. A station wagon
shudders its reverse,
a plum wrinkles
its skin; three nurses
walk their smoke break,
a bird decides no,
paper bag tumbleweeds
tumble. Too much
hangs on a doorknob.
Too many choke
the awnings. Tired water
holds itself up by the curbs;
all that grows in the hardy
filth of the avenue
holds itself up; the dirty hands
and minds, someone
hollering about grace.
Look at that bucket of carrots
outside the deli, glowing
like a lampshade. How can that man,
peeling them in another language,
bear it?
Beside him, pyramids of citrus.
Rows and pyramids and buckets:
all that bounty at eye level. Up above,
nothing at all, as if the sky
has always been imaginary.

Patient S. to Doris

"...uncalled, alive, and sure."
—*Muriel Rukeyser*

Back then the world was full of possibility,
but not the good kind. Lilies held malaria
in their stalks. Down there at my feet
stuck all those silly toes and slow hairs.

So they locked me up
but when I got out, the hairs
still stuck there, patient
as this page.

The noon pond made us calm.
In the wards the light
made our mosquitoed arms
look leprous. I sat by you in group
and you turned your head,
hair delicate as marrow.

All of us said we wanted
everything possible,
but I only believed you.

* * *

Lunch was lovely
when you ate peas.

Peas were lovely near
your mouth. I could imagine

tracking them from stalk
to muscle.

All the voices of the wood
called "Muriel!"

I read in group, and you
were a sucker for it

out of the corner of your mouth.
...not for me, not for me, not for me.

While you talked our hands cut the air
like the shoulder blades

of a stalking lion.
I had three cinderblocks

in the air. *Nothing was speaking to me,
but I offered and all was well.*

* * *

A big sigh for a small body:
It's as if this air was too heavy
for my insides. I'm tired
of rain, sinking and beading,
making itself into marbles,
surviving gas and ice
for the pleasure of cells.
All those water drops wearing
hard hats in the cell factory
make me tired.
I'm tired of food. Chewing.

All the sanity bores me.
Everyone bores me but you;
they are all so many
chortling squirrels.

At night I'm tired of
weather, and go to bed
tracking peas, feeling
them make you again
and again.

Matter

There are the glassy wet balls rolling around in my
face. The hairy holes below flaring into life.
Moist rocks, thin and square and made to
tear and melt things down for swallowing. Strings
sprouting and lengthening from the sphere that holds
all these, strings I gather into a knot of dead
strings with a pretty clip.

We are gangling small things, bits of matter
that don't, and nothing can make us big.
Not the damage, the packing down and tearing up
we do with our spoking fingers and furled brains

and the neck, a stalk that swivels and crooks
and collects its folds of skin that collect blotches
and tears that redden and scar.

Sex can't make us big, or pretty clips, or the damage.
No wonder I want my hard head shell crammed
with stories. Other people's stories, not my Russian
winter, moody cancer, tough bricks of disease. Gangling

and small, my bones crack like cooked clouds
and the stories cook into red marrow.
Without the stories, this shell swivels on its stalk,
empty. I am empty from the clean ceiling of a skull
down to the clean casing of each heel. Without the stories,
I flare ugly into longing, thick packed into every
case and spoke, every cavity, thick and thin space.

September

Strangers come to caretake and her tongue
lies large and quiet in its crook.
Across the street black tin wardrobes and twin
mattresses lean against the old age home

and in next door's empty lot frilled weeds
flatten till they layer like a wing. Spiders rattle
in old leaves looking for food
while the strangers are off provisioning.

They cut loaves for sandwiches
she drags to school
past the Home, where paramedic vans leave
lights running, staining the wall

for split red seconds
want, I want, I want.
She must read the parents' slick-backed
postcards barefoot in the bathroom

after school after food. *They will*
they will. Suppers are bland
on her spicy tongue and at night
the window glosses red

with lights left running
in the rain; from the glass
comes tiny thunder.

Space Exploration

This is about space. Lonely seeds: *wingéd seeds, where they lie cold and low*: seeds I boiled and fried in oil.

Wheat fields under a fat moon. Not sheaves, no sickle yet; just seed heads piled up on straw bodies, perfect little zippers of fruit.

Rice paddies wet silver under a moon. Figs fertilized by the right fig wasp, a mango rotting beneath a tree of mangoes, sweet peas unfurled, sugar snap peas snapping open.

Propellers spin off maples, baobab roots bury themselves in red ground. Red gourds rattle and dry under a fat sun.

***

This is about food,
which has never been
about sustenance.

About space, which
I have never been able
to stare in the face.

About hollows
packed full.

***

The friendly cow, said Stevenson,
I love with all my heart:
She gives me cream with all her might,
To eat with apple-tart.

The friendly girl, I said to him,
I cannot love at all:
I fill me up to hold me tight,
and stuff me like a doll

***

Food is a charcoal pencil
filling me in.

Someone's taken a soft brush
to the underside of my skin,

dipped it in warm syrup
to massage each ball and socket.

When the nerves become sensitive
as a tailor's fingers, food sinks down

and churns into quiet mud.

***

Space is a cavern in my center grown black as the low-humming
danger of stories. A brittle pink gourd as it rattles and dries.

***

This is about
what I can't hold—

face sullied,
whining its way to a wane:

sickle
tight as a cramp

half-circle: the point
at which it begins in the veins

three quarters
swollen to a shine

full
as the moon.

YWCA

She doesn't swim to you.
When you paddle over in orange puffs
she grazes your back with her fingertips.
You grip her arm, rubber-smooth.
You are a tangle of seaweed
around her foot.
A hum below noise, a hat on the stand,
salt on the salt of her tongue.

She treads
black almost forever
in the deep end. Then she will disappear
into a forest of breasts and legs
in the steam room.

Spring 1979

It was a seder, so Grandma's lips were pursed
and her brass purse clips were pursed in her lap
at the table, made L by another fitted in for
cousins and a dozen others. And it was
boring. We didn't think it was supposed to be.
The tzimmes helped because it was so weird.
I was scared of the horseradish. I dreaded
the parsley. Spring was sprung and green
and I was green, about to spring, which
was dreadful like bitter herbs and green
sprigs. My thoughts were all wrong
and would continue to be more and more so
until the matzah had a mind to bind me
prisoner in its crisp, plain walls. The songs,
though, the songs were mournful brown things
that lived and died, unspeakably beautiful.

Forest Floor

Summers we'd watch the carp
leap and arch and sink, tramp
stands of fluorescent mushrooms,
let the blue-bodied bottle
flies settle the branches.

The shade pressed in, a sharp
shimmer. Wasn't grief stuffed
into the marrow of each trunk, wasn't
the trunk sugared in pleasure?
All of it too alive with gorged
bees and anxious seeds.

Doris and I walked through with a bright
frog of color at the corner of each eye.
We were on our way to the edge
of the earth, where it would flatten
and bubble in the pan.

Wednesdays with Mrs. Wolfstein

I should have been more devoted.
Loved the round black notes, the swirl
of treble clef. Her knuckles, big as drawer pulls,
knocked the iron stand in three-four time;

Johan Strauss waltzed her around
the piano bench all year through clouds
of rosin, a curtain of horsehair;
leaned her across the keys.

On stage tonight, black-wrapped bodies
and polished wood make music—glorious,
whorled sounds, electric green reeds
nestled in a silver bowl, sounds I felt

before I was born. The soloist
has worn her chin to callus
for the chance to be what is sad and rich
and endless, what can be lost,

and the loss. Mrs. Wolfstein bends
to scratch a note above the third measure,
her body hums. She is always
inside it. It is always inside her.

Seventh Grade

We float the rink
in Kool & the Gang ovals.
Our skates are heavy off the floor.
Our lips are slick with Bonne Bell.

Soft pretzels turn slowly
under their lamp. Girls lean
on the counter, girls
vulnerable as the backs
of their own necks.

They are in line and I am in line.
They are dreadful and my mouth
is a stuck gate. Somewhere above
the domed roof rests a spine of clouds.
I don't think about it much

but when I do, I'm tired of it.
When I don't, I'm like
the other girls, blank
and pretty as a scarf. Seething
underneath, where I've never been.

Spring Night

Who did I pine for that night,
stumbling the stoop, shoes left tangled
under Katey Margolis' couch?
The door key refused to move the deadbolt,
so when Katey's Dodge squealed off
I sat down hard on the doormat
and watched a cricket saw away into
euphoria, perched on a planter of screaming impatiens.
By the time the right key announced itself,
the cricket's music waxed ecstatic;
how old was Teresa when she found herself
pinned to the ground by madness and joy,
by music, clanking, planets elbowing stars,
doors thrown open—

1988

We didn't know Paul
would die young, but he did.
And Susan. Susan's mother filled
the house with gas, believing her girl
was out. She woke to find her there
but gone. Suffer the children.
Suffer the teens and their sad beer.
Suffer the grown-ups
when there is no such thing.
And Paul, lucky Paul crushing
a last Schaeffer can in his hand
and letting the gun take him
to the garage. He would never
have to drink again.

Doris Can Juggle

three suits of French armor. Three handfuls
of straight pins without losing a one. She can
juggle a bleached blue beached rowboat,
disorientation, and a fig branch, blindfolded.
She can juggle disbelief, a V of geese,
and passionately-tended bonsai. A suit of
French armor, a mound of straight pins, ferns
in a blur of ferns, and a Jewish sunset, and
she can juggle juggling. She is a survivor until
she isn't, a person who handles what is handed
until she can't be that person anymore.

The Real World

A pie-eating contest. Number three
has berries charging down his
bare beefy chest, not a hair
to slow them down.

Stare hard at the smudge
above the fourth rib,
close your eyes:
There's the bush

somewhere in Maine, next to
a thousand others, brown
factories shooting color up
from the roots, the berries

each an eye, each leaf a tiny
mouth sipping light
like milk. Boy
number three pushes up

from oilcloth, O strapping lad,
tugs at his shorts, brushes away
bits of stained crust. Number four
has won, has high-fived three,

has moved on to a vat of mud,
where she will show us how sensual
soil and water can become, when stirred,
when warmed.

16 mm

She won't put down the camera.
The smeared lens ticks
and purrs into the naughty crotch
of an oak, burned pots set to soak, the hint
of gloss on a cloud, and always
me: another grainy subject, flattened
and reeled for love and art. This strip
could wind twice around the earth,
stretch to Venus and back like a pulley.
Somewhere out there tiny squares
bear my likeness, edged
in blurred brown: serious folded hands,
dark teeth, pale lips in the stars.

October

Sally's muzzle is growing white.
Her womb, like mine, has been useless
as a tonsil; like mine, by my choice.

The sugar maples threw down
a yellow rug. The sweet gum
set down swatches. You know

I don't want children. You know
what covers the ground, the lemons,
mittens, goldfish, brown hands.

In a month, two months, they
will be ground into ground.
Their outlines are crisping

like wool on the wheel.
Their outlines are relevant
and crisp, declaring themselves.

Of the Girl

*"The beauty of the girl...is motherhood that has a presentiment
of itself and...becomes anxious and yearns."*
                    —Rilke

He'd imagine, under my clothes
and skin,
the deep wooden bowl, waiting only
for my nod
to fill its hollow with fruit.

Then he would look closer:
brown dust, the face's
slow blink
promising nothing.

What is she, this empty
creature, power
transformed from fate
to cold space?

He wanders his beloved Nature
on soil that lies just above
the angry core of the earth;
just below coils of spent seed pods
smearing the hills.

He imagines the possibilities
of their fruit.

Space Exploration

Silent black and white: the sixth birthday party
of my own mother,
who would not imagine the word *ovary*
for a decade.

A screenful of busty gray women
in a Brooklyn yard ache with
bloodlines, fresh houses, children's
children's children—

the cavern in my center
grows black
as the low-humming danger of stories.

Palms wrinkle into waves just a thin
screen away from the one who has chosen
to be childless: the last of them.

Tell us you are a woman,
tell us you are not for nothing,
beg the women. *Say*
you won't kill us.

***

The sixth birthday party
of my own mother,
who had no idea.

Sugar crust, fiery cake,
elasticked hat. On her father's knee.
Turn around and look at him!
Don't you know he'll be dead
in a year?

***

On her father's knee, my mother squirms, his breath at her ear.
Her mother blows candles with her, back still strong, family alive.
Sugar melts into her tongue.

***

My father's breath at my ear. My father pushing
up horn-rims. My mother, hair back thick and black.
They watch me perform on little legs, mouth
sweet and small as a grape. *Do* something
for the camera! On a tricycle, plunging
through the air as if it weren't there.

***

My sixth birthday party. My mother's
breath at my ear. I will not imagine
the word *ovary* for a decade.

March

Doris is proud to love the fall, proving her
hardy as a burr.
Her favorite food is the peanut, which,
when heavily roasted, tastes like bread
and wine and the ground. Her favorite bird
is the grackle, which looks like
an oil spill, hence like an oil spill
survivor. Her favorite grackle picks
pan dulce by the Hotel Antigua pool,
where white women preen their new
brown babies. ¡*Que linda! Solo agua pura
para mí. Solo hamburguesa para él.*

Doris doesn't want a baby, she wants a bird
thick with petroleum. She wants a brawny
hippie man with a grackle on each shoulder
and despair buried in his right eye,
craving in the left.

Let me bring you a towel, my dirty sweet,
she would say. Let me spoon warm brown
nuts into you. ¡*Que linda! Solo
una nueva vida para mí.*

Because of Stefan

I'm sorry if you have never seen ice imitate the earth's crust,
with its heaves and pocks and blood cell rings. This is nature,
like a man and a woman, or a man and a man. I'm sorry
if you haven't seen it soften its hoop around the skin
of a beech, which is nature, like abortion, or a seed heated
into sprout, or a mother with a mother and their son. On an incline,
on the slick, the climb is tree to tree. It is the nature of some fields
and some women to lie fallow. Some seeds lie in their own smudges
to cool, which is nature, like the cling of girl to girl or glaze to branch.

Doris in Love

When I met you, I ran out of ego. My feet
grew long and flat, nose greasy. My bones
turned to tissue. My brain turned to bone.
I went dolt. What? I said, and my chin broke out.
I'd like to thank you by the hand, I said, voice
like a dropped cork, take you very much.

I knew they were talking about you in every
Union Square in the world. I knew my teeth
were tightening in their sockets. I wanted
a bright blue dependency to grow right in
the middle of you.

Sometimes I am the center of the universe,
but mostly I'm an *and* buried in a book
buried in a library. Sometimes I am just
a little bit worthy. The zip at your crotch
showed a few teeth, gold as a hot day,
the sun a lemon tart cut overhead and
falling, my batch of ogles sweet. O body,
you will cause me to do evil until we part.

The Crush

This is the beginning, and we all know how that is.
She takes your order, no matter what she does for a living.
You flip the cup to signal coffee and it fills with bright
birds. The air is warm as a brown eye.
Her gaze plucks at your ribcage; her gaze sits
in the backseat while you errand. You're filled
with a delicate marrow of fright and charity.
Your charm is a well-heeled little owl.

Soon the harm will come with its patterns. The backseat
gaze becomes oppressive: she's not there out of love,
you've installed her, and she resents it in the rearview.
Two of your heart's chambers had longed for new host,
and the insistence is grating; what a fool you are, and
a clumsy one.

But it's too late. You're a drawer drunk on holding.
A cart drunk on shouldering.

Little Roué

For Sarah Waters

All those days she sat like a wig
in classrooms, eyes roving and lungs
red and toes curling at the girls.
Evenings she made her living
in girls' rooms. Crawled her hands
up their minis. Tinkered with their
bottles and lip gloss and new
bras. Knobby elbows and glazed
thighs and a heart wrapped in a hard
snare drum criss-cross. She stood
on one leg and sang to them, her eyes
two gorillas.

Little roué, waiting for Victorian
Paris to offer you a garretful
of women, one with paint splatters
on her neck, one with ink smudged
under an eye, one with a flask
in her garter belt. The Victorians
will leave the past for you,
beg you to tip the velvet, fill
your red lungs. Will pack up your laughing
and longing into a smart valise and go,
one ending after another ever since.

You Are a Prince

You are a wretch and a leech and a dirty
old man and have been trying to push
inside me for years. Well, come on then.
There's something about the plum warm

air. Usually at this time of day I don't
want to see people. Usually when I'm on
the old swings I think about the man
who stopped his car here and asked me
how to get somewhere and he was naked.
So what. I walked back to the swings
and he drove off with his dumb worm

and his hatchback. That was years ago
and now the seeds are tired of assembling
grass in all this seediness. Come on then.

Smoushound

My heart,
this great Italian
plum cockeyed
in its cage, is the heart
of a thief; still,
on the way home, it
starts to rumble and cook
the instant I picture you
on the sofa, tuned in
to nonsense, or reading
about the Dutch
Smoushound, near
extinction since
World War II.

In a splintery
brown boat
forgotten in an
Amsterdam canal,
a Smoushound reclines.
His pale coat takes
on the light of spongy
clouds sopping up sun.
You lean over the oarlocks
to tell him about himself.

Milwaukee

Downstairs were Al and his nurse wife
and a jumble of kids and cats and Al's neon
art and Princess the tired Doberman and Fred
the iguana, and upstairs were us, two
women with one bed. Those kids wanted
in our space and made themselves at
home when we weren't, okay so long as
when we were they were gone to Fred
warming himself on Al's neons.

Behind our door we filled each other pink
and red, and for a long pretty while that
was enough. It took years for her to finish
with me, and then it was quick over, a
marvel of quick, a five-paragraph essay
kind of final, and there was all that pink
and all that space.

Over

I've lost her.
Is she hiding behind that fruit stand? Or

snorkeling in the Dead Sea, on a quest
for one miraculous fish? Could be

she's wrapped herself in reeds, a performance
art piece on the west coast.

But most likely she's gripping the lip of a moon
crater, legs dangling. I'm yelling up to her,

hands cupped around my mouth, as the firemen
angle the trampoline just so.

Midnight

A handful of cornets declared midnight,
unable to wake an old dog
by the city arch. They spilled knees,
hips, hands through brass bores and bells,
and still she lay there.

Her father was a Briquet Griffon
Vendeen. She inherited his long
white ears. The yellow cornets
waited for her to drift through the gate; still
she lay on her side, as if all the king's men
crooned only to mend her broken body.

That night she let the pulley of notes raise
her as far as she could go, and stayed.

That was the night Orion slipped out of the bowl,
leaving only his glittering belt, unbuckled
into an aching arch,
and the slow creaking of planets.

Over

Now what plum is your tongue
In?

—*Catullus, via Anne Carson*

I would shake her awake but she is done with me.
I would claw into her stomach. I am a harpoon.

She rose round and sweet as birthday cake. She was
skinny in the woods, alone on the bus
with her dry white rolls. She left her words
snagged on the trees. She choked her words down
with the bread. Rode into womanhood
with no words left.

Grief makes me wild and lean
as a safety pin. I'm wild as a harpoon, a thimble.
She's a clean dry package, asleep atop the blankets,
empty eyeglasses on the next pillow, done.

Parting

What is sweet about
it? My breasts are
rock,
hair sore, arms
firewood. The sun is
a sack I'd
like to
smash with a
bat. Under each
racked nail is an
orchestra of
nerves. What is
sweet?
My lungs have
been pulled
through the
gullet and
tied. From
them I dangle
dense,
a lead
plumb.

December

Systems fail. The last time
I looked up, the planets

were gone. Sometimes
I put hand to chest to check
the pump, and it's stopped.

Why is mystery ignoring
us? Bodies around here
are full up with

hollows. Every day I forget
why to risk.

A man cried from his bench,
You must be prepared!
Senses fail. Stars

crush into my ear. They blur
my edges, blunt taste.

The man sings his mystery into
the rusted bellies
of barbecue pits. *That guy*

is crazy, someone says.
Thank god, says Doris.

Parting

Meanwhile everyone here
wears too much skin,
out for everyone to see: hands,
faces exposed and blinding.
We women lounge
about the bar like a stable
of horses. Across the street
buildings are basted
with sunset, dissolving
into space. Meanwhile
my blood is glass.

In a few minutes I will engage
the bartender. We will make
our way to the door marked Authorized
Personnel, and I will do it
for love,
though not his.

Doris Out of Love

I liked you and your
silly bed.
You danced me
around, sailor,
in your stains,
your eye slick
as a ballroom, black
as a cloud. It hit me
like disease. It shook
me like a team of
bones. I watched it
close, upper
and lower lashes
clasped in a warm
handshake. I watched
it open, and it made
bread and fudge
of my belly.

Each moment is one
I am about to lose.
The trick is to stay
tired even after
the lights go out.
You had a dirty
church of a mouth,
and when it touched
me I didn't know what
to do with the paddles
at my wrists. From it
one day you made
the sound a tiny lion
would. From it one
day you frowned
a frown even a firefly
could light. The big gods
and the little would see it,
the big lions and little ones.

Colors

I   Fuchsia

Bloated, unwieldy,
fat velvet

fibers to rub a cheek
then grind a smoke out in.

A Colette heroine
on heroin. Unspellable.

Plump lampshades.
My heart

when you cock
your head at me.

II   Chartreuse

A squint. A pint of over-frozen.
Contracted glands. A squirt.

Nineteen eighty five: Esprit,
Forenza, Ciao, Mia,

Samantha's dollar polish.
Silk wound around a redhead's

white waist. We're drunk on it;
you, me, and the redhead.

III   Puce

Four letters bound together
with straw, the color of wound,

sets of consonant-vowel quitting in pain
after two.

The color of the thought
of teeth against your teeth. I chewed

on that word until I *had* to stop—
Whose gift to language was this?

IV   Ecru

Everything has been washed out of me.
I'm coarse and the ground is coarser.

What is left? No berries, but plenty
of tough wide crisp

stalks. Circle here, aliens! Take the field!
The jaw goes slack. Lips dry

among the stalks. Nothing left
to talk about.

Space

The slow creaking of planets
overhead. Orange pits, smashed
nails and nickels circling.

Doris used to want a single cornet,
but now she wants full orchestra.
She wants an aviary of calling birds

the color of grapefruits and apples.
Tonight, each note dropped a thread for her.
She wrapped them around her fingers

to keep herself here on the ground.
She'd almost grown tired of the music:
the beak of the oboe, the cello's throat.

Maryland

Times someone called to say she was
on her way (a drunk mother, a crazed
mother, a drunk father behind it)
there may have been a bike ride
to meet her in the park, find her
on the drive. There may have been
drink of our own, an incense burn,
or just the climb into cold bed where
now I think I wanted to touch them,
one or more. A cluster of fingers, of
moles, holes that would fill me up
if I filled them up. Sometimes lying
beside one I would fill the tubes
of my brain with cotton, push the
batting through each furl until it was
scoured and empty, none of their sweet
smells or bitter papas, no human
to blight things, to take on poisons
or yearning.

Bride

I haven't smelled my sweat
in months but it's back
with the spring like ticks.
Record high at eighty nine
and my love is still in bed,
unscrubbed. Give me one
reason I shouldn't peel
that dirty shirt, loose
his knees and reach in?
I was a bride, not white
but black and red. Not
a bride, not a pin pressed
between a fitter's lips on
fitting day: I have never
been fit. I black-and-redded
off the rack. This man here
was a groom in green. Why
shouldn't I tear his cotton?
A bodice is for ripping, a groom
suit for popping buttons.
It is tiresome to love this much,
but I will, because the sane
bore me, because he smells
like three Augusts in a row,
because my voice cracked
in half and then quarters
when I spoke down his throat.
I like longing—long for it
even, its popped buttons,
its rips.

In the Park

The frogs were flying and the birds were boating
and it all hummed. Your eyes looked like lentils
so I ate them. You have a beautiful blindness
to you now. Your lips looked like lizards so
I caught them up and sunned them on the rocks.
I love your quiet. Your neck was a spoon
so I balanced it on my knee and smiled into its
wonked mirror. The rest of you is just flesh and
salt, all the regular things, so just let me gather
you up and feel, feel them, feel them.

Paraclausithyron*

So far from the humans you were, a boy dunking ladle to stockpot
of tea back in college, your soul could have been sequestered
with a family of rabbits. It's not your fault.
All you had were pines you planted at fifteen,
so far away you mixed your own seed
into the root grooves.

I am hardly human to you, which works in my favor,
though not enough. Now your ladle makes you drunk,
buries you further. It pickles you, is your temple.

Sweetheart, buried warm in the slurring,
how hard it is for you to love.
You even tire of trees. You tire of roots, floors,
leaves, the want beyond the door,
the want behind the door.

* Lament sung through a lover's locked door.

Strangers

Your brother is ill, mentally ill, some there all along, some blooming as he came of age. You came of age in the bunk below, his shrieks staining the ceiling, grease from his head staining the wall.

You have a trace of his disease, as if he is drowning in what only misted you. The mist makes faces a fog. People are mystery, figures to watch on their plastic fields. Leaves, though, are in sharp focus. Squirrels are, dogs, phoebes. Somehow me.

At the feet of the birches, the mushrooms are on their way out, wrinkled white kneecaps and beaten copper lids listing. You could sing their species and sub-species, nibble at them all day. The rich birches peel themselves just for you. Hummingbirds hum and dive

on your juice. Sometimes I pull you away into a strange house of strangers and your hands dangle, teeth grind until you see a creature winding between the legs.

Full Throttle

Of all the animals at the shelter,
the back of your neck
would find a home fastest.
Something about that mole,
or the two cords muscling
like sharks to the nape.

Your hands, waiting
one cage over, drum
on the slick. They compel,
having done unspeakable things
to bodies, buzzing skin
like a pianoful of strings. No—
like a sit-down mower full throttle.

Enough: What
within you is not perfectly
too much? How about that eye
like a crock of soft slate—
enough. The mind matters,
too, directing matter from its perch
in the quarantine ward,
you autistic devil.

What can I do but lie in bed,
loose my knees, and rub
question mark after question mark
into myself?

In This Way

Let me be a staring terrible moon
of a face for you. Let it be brown-skied
around the dull coin glow of me, the watcher,
the rusty lover, dusk light maker of you. Let
you crack and shudder in my mute light, love,
let you wear this moon coin face of mine
to bed. In this way I can hunt down all
of your pieces and glow them together until
I make you who you are.

Marriage

I'm boring, my stamped
foot and the gavel always
coming down. I'm tired
of myself and poetry but
I'm not tired of dogs, or tv,
or the pleasure of complaint.

I'm not tired of you.
I forgot to write love
poems, then forgot how,
then forgot love
poems themselves,
the cloy of their
syrup, the plump
wax of their cherries.

They liquored me up
to say: Bore
into me like
a beetle, my married
man, like one
of your precious
tools, the bite
of a fat drill bit.

Cold Keen Pole

Time is a fire as tired as a tunnel and as tired
as a verb. Doris feels filled at night with a bitter
mustard. She has given and got as hard as the rest,
a princess of chafe, a sorcerer of sore and apprentice
to fault. She has winked while the moon rolled its sour eye.

Damn it, she wants hope like everyone else does, to peek
corners, dream calls. She's ticklish with want. But at night
she is filled with a bitter juice that goes through her like
a cold silver pole, a high silver wind. It is keen, and she
is keen on it. It's gulped down her tubes like a vinegar joke.

Wasting goes through, hurt does, waste.
All along her outsides, time is a fire, a lonely light
spent so fast it makes her sick. *The watch*
kept on cutting time
with its little saw, Neruda said.

If Only

The Book of Gretchen is a downer.
　　　　　　　　—Gus Mueller

On foot, on bicycle, via messenger: what a day.
The soy in flower, the weather over and under
like hands, a stand of successful trees leaning in.

Doris and I lie in the soy, minds blank as a bean,
let the leaves gentle, let the bugs settle
their wings. Cells dive in the soil, but also

burst and dry. I want to save my
darlings, but there is no such doing.
That is the Hudson, heading in the wrong

direction, finally free of salt. Beaten
grass stretches to the plate
of water, where the bridge is wrapped orange

in construction. Men are busy making it
well, doting on its north.
Having been born, says Doris,

is not reason enough to be kept alive.
Having been born, I say,
does not mean holy

or even good. A woman wanted.
A man may have. So I was born.
So what!

I'd like unscrew my arms and legs and head
from my torso, says Doris. I'd like a button
above the jaw to trigger the sleep of the blank.

The bridge leads to the Catskills, the sediment
of another range. Recycled mountains.
Four hundred million years ago, this was reef,

the Bahamas. What is a long time? No wonder
I want to end already,
to fossilize in a press of sand.

Doris (Cardiology 14 E)

They had been jammed into their bodies without knowing why.
—Anne Sexton

My bones are in one hospital room,
soft tissue another. I don't mind the blood; I like
to see it on this side of my skin for a change.
My sack of skin packed with red and brown organs,
like clown parts stuffed into a duffel. Sometimes
I sponge down my skin suit until it is clean, with nothing
from the inside soaking through.

I don't mind the passage of time; it means
I can enjoy hindsight. Thoughts are elastic: A picnic
at the botanic gardens: Starched petals, starchy pistils,
floury moths, all here to perform, little do they know.

I've probably been more alone,
but I can't think when. I can't think why
someone would create a child.

Oho, Doctor! Come monitor my lumbering heart
for signs of disease. From time to time it growls
like a bird. From time to time it falls like a rose head.
You are qualified to scribble such things in my chart;
my own mother let you work alongside
her awkward brown heart until they dumped me,
a bucket of proteins, into the world, to live and dry
under the planets.

All around the world, the regular people
are growing bone shards in their bellies.
The eye sockets are digging themselves
out. The meat starts. The eruption of hope
around cord blood. They start to punch
in the sixth month. Some things come later,
arbitrarily. Teeth, for instance. A hard
skull. Hair. Some things are there

from the beginning, like skin and saliva,
like punching.

They will become us, and why? The regular
women want to stick something
to themselves. Grow tiny new suits
of skin. Grow organs fitted like countries
into the chest in their chest. Enough!
Let me slough,

Doctor. I know what you're thinking behind
your masks and charts, same as I am: *I can unravel you,*
unwrap the meal of you, unshutter your sweet little
house. What are you blinking for? Slide
your eyes closed! Don't bruises swim
behind our lids? Doesn't yellow script float there:
I'm sorry?

To Abortion

Thank you for thinning
our terrible ranks.
I'm sorry about the tiresome
lack of frankness,
the guilts and sobbings.
We should be kinder to you.
I have not used you—
I am too careful—
and so have stayed quiet.
Let them be quiet now,
their bitter sputters. What
do they know
who could never
know? How blessed I am:
should I need you,
you will come into me
and I will be cleaned
out, saved.

Anita

You have taken on various gods
through the years, handholds
on a glass cliffside. Once it was Jesus
in the guise of a young Angolan
woman in L.A. They strapped you
down and rolled you away from her,
no gods any help at all.

Now you want to grow a person,
someone to tend your manic
laugh. Your sweet husband is
willing, and that is the mystery
of the heart and the blood
in the heart calling for more
of itself.

Your child will take on various
gods through the years. The sadness
will start deep in her face. Her
chest will fill with cold water
she will work to warm

day in and out, in and out, walking it
along the hurt beaches, the pounded
crust of the continent. Sometimes
she will stay locked in bed.
Sometimes they will strap
her down, no gods any help
at all.

Don't make her.

It Is Green

...He looks at the leaf—it is green—
And says with a flat black leather gesture:
"Never again."
                    —*Randall Jarrell*

I   April

It's all the ooze, says Doris. Desperate.
All the bursting underbrush. There's no

solace in the thickening.
In the fiddleheads waiting

to slide
open.

No spent brown seeds,
red hands, sweet gum swatches

on the ground, no rattles
or dry wings, just the tight

green purses desperate
before they even have

mouths. Doris is in a corner,
hiding hers.

II   November

Chestnuts, rattling pods, a lawn chair
rusting luxuriously in the weeds.

Doris leaning back, lids to the last
sun, fiddle-string veins running

bold up each splayed arm.
Not alone,

she tells the grouse. Deliciousness.
And only looking forward

to. Stationary spinning trees,
air on their backs,

fiddle-string bark curls bold
up the branches, splayed,

cold squirrels curled in the chinks,
the clickalong of dry petals skating.

.

Great Blasket Island

The ferry docked and we
climbed past panicked rabbits
to high fog, but Dave wound down
to the coves where seals surfaced
in the drizzle. He saw a ghost

and wrote it up in caps,
spelled—out of the soup
of ghosts and the tough
fibers of his chest and the delicate
factory of his brain—his father,

the cavern, the tunneling well
his father flew from,
plunged into. He wrote the coves,
the Sheffield mill
where he'd spent half his life,

where he'd punch in Monday.
I know because he unfolded the poem,
all creases, at the Tralee bus station
before he boarded with ghosts the color
of sand. He put it in my hand

because he was looking for
a blessing, and there is no such thing.

Child

Thorn teeth gnaw white bread and ketchup.
Instant audition on my haunches; her sack cheeks
turning away. Hands tacky on the cup.
Smell of soured cream, shriveled leeks.

Her mind a dusk mushroom. Arms up in puppet-jerks.
Eyes narrow and narrow, jaw drops
for the scream. Under her hair lurks
new hair, different skull, new hands on cups.

So new, imperious, dumb.
How much time she's left: to shed,
gather tight, peel.

Market

Behind the counter, sneaking
almonds and slivers
of block chocolate smashed
in back with a hammer,
Doris is regal, imperial, in
charge! Can tell rolled oats
from steel-cut at fifty
feet. Can smell the age
of cheddar. The women
trust her with their food
stamps, platinum cards, black
eyes. And when she steps down
to mop alone at night, she reaches
over to fill her hand
with a shower of gold dried
apricots. Boxes flattened crisp,
grate pulled down,
the road a flat roll
of licorice. On the sidewalk
she looks up at the stamped
punched eye of the moon.
It's scary, its haughtiness,
how much it loves its bruises.
How dare you, she says, and pushes.

Tony's Goodbye

I wanted to tell you without a rope.
There were no other means.
The day I stood on crates, groped
the top shelf for the coil, it wasn't about dreams
thwarted, or the tough pitted skin of the heart.
And should you think what I've ended, this task,
was from lack of loving you, only think of my art:
how I stuffed my breath with you as I blew into the glass.
Still, the ground's littered with electric split
seconds, leaf skeletons, empty cups,
salt, driftwood bones. And so I pushed off it,
boosted myself up.

Ugly Wheel

Sometimes Doris is eight foot six, a mad
giantess in boots, a monopoly on
Bigger Than, a bearer of mixing-bowl
ashtrays and dozen-glazed snacks.

Sometimes she plays the spoons on
Venice Beach, an Older Than, a More
Tired Than, tips in a pie tin,
apples in a bag for last.

Sometimes a girl. A fluffy chick snapped
up by a foxy broad. Sometimes a foxy
broad. Sometimes her head is crammed
with other people's stories, sometimes

it is its own ugly wheel. She flies
sometimes, tunnels others. Sometimes
she zippers, sometimes pops buttons.
She is rich sometimes, red sometimes.

A dabber, a dipper, a plunger, a drowner.
Sometimes all of the above.
Sometimes none of the below.
A wracked wreck, a soothed silk

saint. A wretched wench, a slurring
sack. Sometimes it is alright that she
will watch her skin turn to paper.
Sometimes it is dumb and hard to love

fragile things: lives and dogs, a pretty
case stuffed with half her memories.
Sometimes it is alright to operate
under her assumption that she might

keep living. Sometimes she Mozarts,
sometimes Mos Defs. Sometimes

she operates as if she won't last long
enough for a wound to heal.

*It doesn't cost anything to just
think it*, she always says.

Bird

Doris takes off her shoes
and folds and wraps
herself so small she fits
into the lung of a bird.

All of her had been tired. Nervous system,
circulatory—blood lurking in the pink glossy
heart, blue glossy ribbons—all the systems
stuffed into their tube of skin.

Her soul was tired from making time
over and over. Of giving time away.
All the systems, all that time
packaged on soles slim as pages.

So she fit herself into the lung
of a bird. Here she is now,
pumping song through air.
None of us can sing like that.

Somewhere Along the Way

A tuba floats in the arms of a man
in sneakers on wet cobbles, its shine
the color of frozen gasoline; a trumpet
sounds the sound of cream-yellow tulips
thrown wide open; firemen lean
on mailboxes, boys let go of each other
across from old women who play the radio
all day, from stained cooks smoking:
intake, exhale, like the brass
men, cheeks stuffed with candy,
sugar spun on air and tar
and bell, lips disappearing
into notes disappearing into black
slicks, memory, flicked ash;
music two seconds old and bruising
the weather, three seconds old rich
as sugar thrown wide to the bowl of planets.

About the Author

Gretchen Primack's poems have appeared in *The Paris Review, Prairie Schooner, The Massachusetts Review, FIELD, Antioch Review, Ploughshares,* and other journals. She's the author of a previous poetry collection, *Kind* (Post Traumatic Press, 2013) and a chapbook, *The Slow Creaking of Planets* (Finishing Line, 2007). Primack has worked as a union organizer, working women's advocate, and prison educator. Also an advocate for non-human animals, she co-wrote *The Lucky Ones: My Passionate Fight for Farm Animals* (Penguin Avery, 2012) with Jenny Brown. She lives in the Hudson Valley. Her website is www.gretchenprimack.com.

Other Recent Titles from Mayapple Press:

Sally Rosen Kindred, *Book of Asters*, 2014
        Paper, 74pp, $15.95 plus s&h
        ISBN 978-1-936419-34-0
Stephen Lewandowski, *Under Foot*, 2014
        Paper, 80pp, $15.95 plus s&h
        ISBN 978-1-936419-32-6
Hilma Contreras (Judith Kerman, Tr.), *Between Two Silences/ Entre Dos Silencios*, 2013
        Paper, 126pp, $16.95 plus s&h
        ISBN 978-1-936419-31-9
Helen Ruggieri & Linda Underhill, Eds., *Written on Water: Writings about the Allegheny River*, 2013
        Paper, 108pp, $19.95 plus s&h (includes Bonus CD)
        ISBN 978-1-936419-30-2
Don Cellini, *Candidates for sainthood and other sinners/ Aprendices de santo y otros pecadores*, 2013
        Paper, 62pp, $14.95 plus s&h
        ISBN 978-1-936419-29-6
Gerry LaFemina, *Notes for the Novice Ventriloquist*, 2013
        Paper, 78pp, $15.95 plus s&h
        ISBN 978-1-936419-28-9
Robert Haight, *Feeding Wild Birds*, 2013
        Paper, 82pp, $15.95 plus s&h
        ISBN 978-1-936419-27-2
Pamela Miller, *Miss Unthinkable*, 2013
        Paper, 58pp, $14.95 plus s&h
        ISBN 978-1-936419-26-5
Penelope Scambly Schott, *Lillie was a goddess, Lillie was a whore*, 2013
        Paper, 90pp, $15.95 plus s&h
        ISBN 978-1-936419-25-8
Nola Garrett, *The Pastor's Wife Considers Pinball*, 2013
        Paper, 74pp, $14.95 plus s&h
        ISBN 978-1-936419-16-6
Marjorie Manwaring, *Search for a Velvet-Lined Cape*, 2013
        Paper, 94pp, $15.95 plus s&h
        ISBN 978-1-936419-15-9
Edythe Haendel Schwartz, *A Palette of Leaves*, 2012
        Paper, 74pp, $14.95 plus s&h
        ISBN 978-1-936419-14-2

For a complete catalog of Mayapple Press publications, please visit our website at *www.mayapplepress.com*. Books can be ordered direct from our website with secure on-line payment using PayPal, or by mail (check or money order). Or order through your local bookseller.